Marketing 33AD

The Path to a Perfect Plan

Donald W. Barden

Marketing33AD

Printed by:
90-Minute Books
302 Martinique Drive
Winter Haven, FL 33884
www.90minutebooks.com

Published in the United States of America

Book ID: 161103-00600

ISBN-13: 978-1-945733-39-0
ISBN-10:194573339X

*To Lisa, Jake, Luke and Nick
God's perfect gift in my life.*

Here's What's Inside...

Introduction

Marketing33AD!

Several years ago, when I was on Wall Street, I was asked to perform a study based on research I was compiling while working on my PhD. I had this incredible idea that I desperately wanted to prove, and one I will never forget. I happened to work for one of the most gregarious CEOs of the time—a great man who had vision and the ability to see things to completion. We were close and I felt he looked at me as a rising star, but a bit like a "grandson" as well. That's why his reaction to my idea burned so deeply in my mind.

When I presented my thesis to him, he looked at me and he said, "Wow Kid. That's one of the greatest ideas I've ever heard."

My heart leaped with joy and pride.

"So, we are approved to start?" I asked.

That's when everything went south.

 "Start if you want," he said, "but I can never fund something like this."

"Why can't you fund it?" I replied in shock. "You just told me that it was the one of the greatest ideas you have ever heard."

That is when he told me one of life's and business's simple truths.

"It's really simple." He said, "I have to look at every project with a focus on our potential to profit, then to replicate and scale it. If there's no foreseeable way to replicate this idea or scale it, then we can't profit, therefore we cannot do it."

He went on.

"In turn, as much as it excites me and I really want to know your conclusion, it's not anything we can profit from as a business. It's not who we are. It's not what we do." He said, "Don't worry, kid, it's still a great idea."

He went on to say, "Go back and think of something different. Tell us what it is that you can study from a different approach of the same concept. Maybe there's something else in the same area you are looking."

I went back to him a week or two later and said, "Sir, there is something else going on with this project. Whenever I travel around the world, I have the pleasure of working with top-tier performers.

Best of all, I have observed something special about these elite professionals ; whomever I am working with, no matter what language they're speaking, no matter what culture they're living in, they all seem to be similar."

"It appears they are acting and behaving in the exact same manner as each other. I have noticed that if you strip out culture, take away languages, and remove all social specifics, you simply have human beings talking to other human beings. Yet, there was something more. I have noticed that these top performers had something in common, while seemingly having nothing in common."

We had studied people all over the world. We worked with dairy farmers in Italy and tortilla manufacturers in Mexico. We collaborated with cell phone distributors in Eastern Europe as the communist bloc was breaking down, and emerging entrepreneurs in China. I worked with many types of people around the world, and there was at least superficially nothing in common with any of them. This was a long time before Facebook and LinkedIn, so there wasn't the chance for them to be connected on social media. There was no reason any of these folks could be brought together, yet they seemed to be exactly the same when they were performing at the highest levels.

I told my CEO about this and said, "Look, there seems something unique about this. I believe that there's a secret sauce that these top-tier performers are using or doing, and if we can figure it out, then we'll be able to profit from it and replicate it. I want to embark on a study that will allow us to discover its truths, prove it, self-inject it, and scale it to the marketplace."

The bottom line, I believed, was that the secret of the world's most impactful leaders could be proven, and would definitely be marketable.

In the end, that study became known around the world as The Perfect Plan. It has reached 39 countries and has impacted lives around the globe.

Yet, true to form, I never gave up on my original idea. I knew that even though it might not have been the business option necessary for profits and scale, it had to be revealed.

So, in a not so secretive way, we ran a similar study for my original theory at the exact same time as The Perfect Plan. It was based on the original hypothesis that I had taken to my CEO, which he felt was necessary to reject.

We called this study, Marketing 33 AD.

The hypothesis was simple.

I believe that the Apostles of Jesus Christ had a marketing plan; they didn't just hang out with a great teacher for three years, and then after he left, aimlessly wander around the earth until they figured out how to live what their great teacher had taught.

No. I believed there was more.

Jesus had taught them very detailed specifics while he was with them for those three short years. They took that teaching, and they carried it forward.

The challenge that we had to overcome as researchers was that we (like everyone else) were taught a certain way to read, envision, and interpret things. We all had heard certain stories as little children, 'Sunday School' versions of the stories which became embedded into our brains, and we carried these versions with us our entire adult lives.

My team and I were intrigued and knew something was there.

Something was missing.

The truth was hiding from us.

At first, we couldn't figure out where the missing link was, or what it might have been, but we knew it was there.

So, as scientist, we began to look at the story from a historical view to say, "Something big had to happen that prepared this movement to last for 2,000 years and to this day, maintain a global 1/3 global market share."

There is no way that in just three years' time, walking around several small villages telling really cool stories filled with metaphors of the time, they could've accomplished what they did without a divine wind.

In other words, they had to have a plan, a Perfect Plan.

We did this study in a manner that allowed us to reverse-engineer the Bible's New Testament with a focus on the realism of the stories context. We also studied the Old Testament, but our focus stayed primarily on what the Apostles of Jesus Christ were doing, and what they might have been "thinking". In other words, did their actions speak louder than their words?

We said to ourselves, "Is it possible they had a plan and a marketing agenda given to them by Jesus that allowed them to move forward, so they could accomplish their goals?"
To follow this theory, we began by taking the Sunday School version of these stories out of our minds and started to re-look at these stories as adults. We forced ourselves to erase our past opinions and thoughts, and look at them as professionals, scientists, and most of all, humans living in a real world.

We discovered that would take some time. "Sunday School" had etched its mark in our brains deeper than we had anticipated.

Here's the good news. When completed, we had the ability to look at life through two separate lenses. Both studies, the Perfect Plan and Marketing33AD, were complete and each proved a point.

After all was said and done, without any communication between the two studies during the research period, we took both studies, Marketing33AD and The Perfect Plan, flipped them over, and realized their conclusions were exactly the same.

It turns out, the Perfect Plan proved there is a formula that elite, top-tier performers around the world follow in order to have the highest impact on their business, their life, their relationships, and in everything that they do.

Yet, there was also a formula hidden within the Apostles' methodology that dictated how they spoke, how they communicated, and even how they prayed. It was even true when Jesus Christ himself said his prayers.

Here is the fun part.

Both studies proved that the methodology of the world's elite performers was exactly the same as that of the Apostles.

Now, you might say to yourself, "Does that mean all these top performers are Christians?"

No. They weren't all Christians; nowhere close.

We do believe some of these high-impact leaders had learned things through their childhood which caused them to act a certain way, but as a group they were vastly different people with this one common denominator:

They believed in serving others before themselves.

We found that some of them simply stumbled onto it, maybe a few just did it because it was the right thing to do, but however they got there, they were doing exactly what Jesus had taught the Apostles to do; Serve Others.

That's what this book, *Marketing AD 33* is about.

It takes you back to that original hypothesis and asks the question: have we been reading these stories the wrong way for all of these years?

What are they really trying to teach us?

As we begin to take a look at the Bible from a different perspective, we ask that you open your mind to a new way of thinking. Keeping in mind, it's just a first step.

As a teacher and a trainer, I can give you a great biblical history lesson on what the Apostles were doing, but it's going to be hard to understand if you don't give your mind permission to reconsider what you might think you already know.

The purpose of this book is actually a little bit different from a traditional Bible study. In this case, we want to remove the Sunday School versions of these stories from your mind. We're going to take those childhood tales you have grown up listening to in a certain way, remove them, and rethink them as an adult.

In this book, as a first step in rethinking your thinking, I want to share with you three stories that you may or may not know. Whether you're a Christian or not, you probably heard these stories at some point. They represent wonderful childhood morality plays, yet I ask that you consider looking at them as an adult. I also challenge you to continually ask yourself a simple question.

"Why?"

"Why would they have done it this way?"

"What does this story really mean?"

"What would I have done if this was about me?"

Our hope is, with the help of this book, you find yourself intrigued enough to go back and do one thing, and one thing only: read the Bible.

If you do, I ask that you read it from cover to cover like a novel. It is the only way to discover one of the most amazing stories ever written. Not only will it be the most astonishing story you've ever read, you will find it has a very specific purpose and intent. In the end, it is a textbook for human life. It tells you step by step how to create, grow, and accomplish wonderful things.

So, that's what this is all about, and I hope you pick up the Bible and read it as an adult, approaching it as a novel, and take things out of it that will allow you to impact the world, serving others.

Cheers to your Perfect Plan, and welcome to Marketing33AD!

Don Barden

Marketing 33 AD, In the Beginning...

Ok, let's start in the very beginning.

The study began with how we came to start thinking so differently about this concept of an adult's view of Sunday School. The very first question we ran into was simple enough and was based on the guy who started it all.

"Who was this guy named Jesus?"

We looked at the original pictures, and began the discovery process critically asking tough, but logic questions. The first being:

"Okay look, if he really went around the Middle East wandering in and out of small towns teaching his followers, and if people around the world are still shadowing these movement 2,000 years later, then there must be something to it. But if we're going to approach this narrative as adults, we've got to be very, very honest with ourselves."

The first thing that we asked was, "Who would follow this guy? Who would go out there and prescribe to his teaching even if it meant a death sentence under the Roman guard?" We looked at this first picture, and it was the European, blonde-haired, blue-eyed Jesus. Now, if anybody has ever studied anything about that area of the world, or at least turned on your TV at night and watched what's going on around there today, you might have noticed we all look a little bit different. One of the great creative things God did was to make the world a smorgasbord of people. The variety is amazing. Every size,

shape, color, and flavor you can imagine exist among us as a people. We are, simply put, different.

Now, we do know that some people from certain areas look a certain way. We also know there's no way Jesus looked like this, yet for some reason, in Sunday School, they burn this image into your brain.

To be straight forward and truthful, Jesus was a first-century Palestine Jew living in areas surrounding Jerusalem.

Would he have had blonde hair and blue eyes? Uh, no.

Would have had long hair? Probably not.

Yet no matter the length or color of his hair, we do know one thing. He would've had something very, very special going on to have attracted as many people as he did.

This painting was famously done so that the Europeans of the time could look at it and feel safe and comfortable. They turned Jesus into a mid-century European in order to control those who needed hope, and the church was the only place they felt safe. With that in mind, Jesus began to look just like them with his blonde hair and blue eyes.

Now, you've got to say yourself, "How about this guy?"

I call this guy the "Holier than Thou Jesus". He's holding his hands out and he is basically saying, "I love you, but don't touch me. I'm holy."

That's consistent with the Cecil B. DeMille versions of Jesus from the 1940s, '50s, and even into the '60s classic Hollywood

movies, like *Ben-Hur* and *The Ten Commandments*. Nothing is obviously wrong with this depiction, but from a marketing point-of-view, and simply from an adult's point-of-view, would you follow one of those guys?

Would you go to the ends of the Earth for someone who refuses to touch you and is so unapproachable?

Would you risk your life for a belief system because some guy who says, "I love you, but don't touch me," asks you to do something?

I don't think most of us would follow those guys, nor do I believe the Apostles would either.

We were looking at this concept in total disbelief saying to each other, "Okay, this is difficult. If it is 2,000 years ago and you're going to start the Christian movement, you've got to start with this guy named Jesus, yet all these images burned into our brains as children are in conflict with what we know as an adult."

The blue-eyed, blonde-haired Jesus?

No.

The holy I-love-you-but-don't-touch-me Jesus?

No.

That is when something beautiful happened.

Around the late fall of 1995, in the middle of our study, I stumbled upon something totally by accident.
One Sunday morning, randomly flipping channels on TV, I came across an actor being interviewed about a movie he had just filmed titled *Matthew*.

During the interview, the actor, Bruce Marchiano, talked about the techniques he utilized as he approached his character, Jesus. He wanted to immerse himself into the character as he, a professional actor, would for any other role. He said to himself, "I've got all this stuff burnt into my mind as a child, but now I've got to look at this differently."

"I've got to get this right, and I need to approach this man I'll be playing the way any actor would by 'getting into' a character." So, he started studying Jesus, and the things around the time of the story he found interesting.

In the movie *Matthew*, Bruce Marchiano spoke the exact words that are printed in the Bible, as written in the New International Version (NIV English). Nothing was added to the dialogue, but in a change from past performers of Jesus, Bruce approached it as a type of Broadway play, and ejected the Cecil B. DeMille version out of his head.

Bruce questioned, "How is this person Jesus, going to attract so many people? How is this guy going to say these words and make it happen?"

So Bruce approached the character from two angles: First, as an actor, he added laughter and expression. Second, as a living, breathing person. He wanted to show a man who loved people and was not afraid to call them to follow him. Most importantly, if you look at this picture, you'll notice something incredibly different: he has this giant smile on his face. When Bruce created the character of Jesus he wanted to portray, he said, "Look, there's no way Jesus went out into the crowds and didn't smile, and didn't hug, and didn't get dirty with the people." In order to attract people, Jesus had

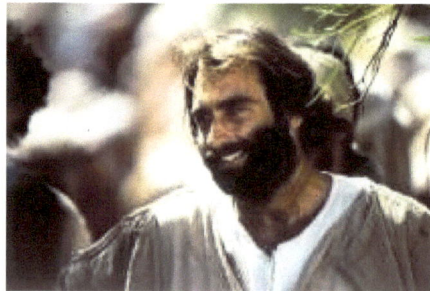

to become one of them. He had to have emotion and most of all, he had to be approachable.

One of my favorite scenes in the movie is when he healed the blind man. In the iconic scene, the blind man is cured and can see for the first time in his life. Amazingly, he looks up and the first person he sees is the one who healed him, Jesus.

In past recreations of the story, Jesus does the holier-than-thou thing (The - I love you but don't touch me Jesus) from the 1950s movies just before he says with monotone low voice, "You are healed. Now go forth to the temple as Moses told you to do."

Thankfully, when it was time for Bruce to play the role, that didn't happen.

"There's no way it would've happened like that," he said. "Think about it this way. This guy's been blind his entire life. He opens his eyes for the first time, and who does he see? He sees Jesus. Now, would it have been a shock if he got this 'blond haired holier than thou' Jesus, or the 'I-love-you-but-don't-touch-me' Jesus, or better, what if he saw the real Jesus - one that had a big smile on his face?"

Bruce remarked, "Let's act this thing out as if it's a play. Let's don't change a single word, but let's make sure we've got the proper emotion in it."

If you go back and watch Bruce doing the scene, once the blind man opens his eyes, he starts laughing and crying, as he sees this wonderfully pleasant man with a giant smile on his face. In fact, he's smiling so big his eyes are actually smiling. Once the blind man sees Jesus, he actually runs toward him with excitement and tackles him. They laugh, and they fall onto the ground rolling around in dirt embraced in a wonderful loving hug, when Jesus, instead of saying with a low bellowing voice the "Go forth and do this," he (Bruce) looks at him with a laughing smile full of excitement for him and says, "Now go forth. You can go to the temple and do just like Moses told you to do."

In other words, Jesus had a smile on his face, and he was celebrating for the man who was once blind, because now he could do something that he was not allowed to do in the past, he could go to the Temple and pray. The emotion at that moment would not have been 'holier than thou'; it would have been a joyful celebration with a giant smile. It would have been with warmth, and laughter. It would have been with a glitter in his eye, so when the man who was once blind went and told the world what had happened to him, he would've told them about that Jesus—a man who loved him and shared the moment with him as a human, with a laugh and a smile.

The first thing we had to do was figure out who this warm and welcoming guy was, who and started a movement and changed the world. We also needed to know why, for some unknown Sunday School reason, we had another version of this guy burned into our brains.

As miracles would have it, now, on that wonderful Sunday morning flipping channels and stopping on a random interview, we found it.

Thank you, Bruce Marchiano.

Thank you for approaching your character differently that tradition might have it, because you cleared the path to our study. You removed the fog from our heads and allowed us to proceed with reliable research. We could now look at the Bible and say, "Now, we get it. Now, we know who the main character's ultimately going to be. The foreshadowing of it was epic. This real-life Luke Skywalker kind of guy, the man of the Bible, the man we all wanted to love but never had the chance to see him as he really was. We now know this guy, and we know he's there on the pages with a smile on his face. That is a game changer and that is what makes it so interesting."

So now we start with Marketing33AD and a few of our favorite stories. We are going to share with you a few formidable and mind-blowing parts from our study, so you can go out there with courage and say, "I'm going to read the Bible, and I'm going to have a different mindset and a different understanding. I am finally going to "get it'."

Full disclosure, I am not a theologian. I am a classically trained economist, but I specialize in behavioral economics, which means I care more about why people make the decisions they do than I care about yield curves and interest rates. Now, if you want to talk about those things, we can do it all day long, but guess what? It's a bit boring.

To me, the way people make decisions is cool. It is what makes us as humans, special.

I tell you this because I had a unique and unfair advantage when I started reading the Bible as an adult, and as a novel. As I was reading, I was also looking at why people did what they did, and as trained, I always asked "Why?"

As you read through the following stories, and you started asking questions yourself, your mind will begin to open up to something beautiful: a story that will change your life and your world.

Genesis 4

Every good story has a beginning, middle and an end. The Bible is no different.

As we begin our focus on the Apostles, we find that they are actually at the end of the story yet, they must have known how the beginning and the middle had played out. That's why it was important to us as researchers to understand the entire story, if we are to fully comprehend their roles.

As we began our search in the beginning of the story, something magical popped out; something we never expected.

If you're going to read the Bible, as many people do at some point during their life, then you're going to start with the story called Genesis. It's a cool narrative that is made up of a lot of those famous "Sunday School" tales. It has several of the children's action stories full of metaphors we find repeated in classic literature throughout the ages. If you start in the beginning, I invite you once again to think as an adult, but fair warning, it will be hard.

In the beginning, there's Adam and Eve. There's a fig leaf. There's a snake (we think) and an entire lot of human history crammed into a few short chapters.
With all of these things going on, i.e., the fall of man from God's grace, an undiscovered land of pure delight, and a conversation between deities we still can't totally comprehend, the Bible very quickly moves to one of its key stories: that of two brothers named Cain and Abel.

Now, Cain and Abel were born from their parents, Adam and Eve, and one (Cain) killed the other (Abel). Cain was punished and banished from the land of delight (The Garden of Eden) by being forced into a foreign land.

It's an interesting study.

In the text below, you'll see the complete story from the Bible's text. We've used the New International Version, which is modern English, so it will unfold in a way that you can read and understand.

As you read, I want you to focus on the words that we've italicized and the comments in parentheses'.

Genesis Chapter 4 New International Version translation:

Adam made love with his wife, Eve, and she became pregnant and gave birth to a son named Cain. Eve said, "With the help of the Lord, I've brought forth a man." Later, she gave birth to his brother, Abel. Now, *Abel kept flocks, and Cain kept the soil.*

(That's an interesting concept. This is where you start asking "Why?"'. One of the sons has been given a job, and that job is then to watch their animals. The other son has been told to farm the land, and take care of the soil. You have a cattle rancher, in modern terms, and you've got the person who's out there farming.)

Through the course of time, Cain brought some of his fruits of the soil *(in other words, what he had farmed)* to the Lord. Abel brought some of his offerings that were fat portions and some of the firstborns of his flock. *The Lord looked in favor at Abel.*

(Abel, the guy who cared for the animal, had basically brought God a steak dinner and for whatever reason, God liked it more than the fruits. He never say's He was against the fruits that Cain had brought, but he really liked that steak, or the fat portions of it. So Cain was angry and downcast.)

Then, the Lord said to Cain, "Why are you angry? Why is your face downcast? If you do what's right, you'll be accepted."

(In other words, just do your job. It's okay. I'm not judging anybody here.)
"If you do not do what's right, sin is crouching at your door. It desires to have you, and you must rule over it."

(In other words, "Look, if you start going around with a bad attitude, then guess what? You're going to get sucked down a path that you don't want to go to.)

Then, Cain said to his brother, "Let's go out into the fields, where I work." While they were in the fields, Cain attacked his brother, and he killed him.

(Now, that's important for many reasons. This is the first murder mystery of the Bible, and believe me, there's plenty of sex, drugs, and rock and roll later in the Bible. If you read it, it would be fascinating…

Then, God shows up.)

…and the Lord said to Cain, "Where's your brother, Abel?" Cain says, "I don't know. Am I my brother's keeper?"

(One of the greatest quotes of all time. He's saying, "Hey, I'm not responsible for the guy. He's an adult. He's his own man out there. Why are you asking me where he is?")

Then the Lord said, "What have you done?
Listen, your brother's blood cries out to me from the ground."

(In other words, "Look, I know what happened here. Now, guess what? You're going to be punished.")

"*You are now under a curse*, and you will be driven from this ground, which opened up its mouth and received your brother's blood." He said, "When you work the ground from now on, it's no longer going to yield crops to you. You'll be *a restless wanderer of the earth*."

(Now, that was really interesting. We started asking "why?"

Why would he be a restless wanderer of the earth?

What does that really mean?

We believe it means he's going to be a caveman. For whatever safe environment existed inside the boundaries of Eden, now he's being cast out and into an unsafe world. He's going to be restless, he's not going to get a lot of sleep, and he's going to be a wanderer, he's going to constantly move around. He's going to be on his own.

Whereas he lives on a farm now, where they have livestock and produce, he's being cast out. He's going to be a homeless wanderer, restless forever, out in the world.

Cain was terrified.)

Cain said to the Lord, "My punishment is more than I can bear." "Today, you're driving me from this land, (*my safe environment*), and I will be hidden from you, (*the one who keeps me safe*), and I will be a restless wanderer of the earth. Whoever finds me is going to kill me. (*"I can't survive out there," is what he's saying.*)

Then the Lord said, "That is not so. If anyone kills you, they'll suffer vengeance seven times over." Then the Lord put a mark on Cain, so that anyone who found him would not kill him.

(We don't know what "a mark" means, but whatever it is, he was leaving his safe environment, yet there was something on him that said, "Don't mess with this guy.")

Cain went out of the Lord's presence, and he lived in the land of Nod, east of Eden. Cain made love to his wife, and she became pregnant and gave birth to Enoch. Then, they built a great city, and they named it after him. Enoch had…

"wah wah wah and blah blah blah and blah blah blah."

This is where most people stop reading the Bible, because you get into what we call "the begottens".

"The begottens" is another word for sex, but they don't like to say that in the Sunday School version of the Bible. The reality is, all these wandering people start having children, and the Bible, because it was purposeful and important at the time, lists the chronological names of these family members. Back then, we didn't have LinkedIn, we didn't have Facebook, we didn't have Ancestry.com, so it was important to know whom you came from and that's why it was always written down.

It is a family tree for a large portion of the population, and they took enormous efforts to continually remind people for thousands of generations to come. This may seem cool and interesting to some, but it's incredibly boring to read.

As you do read through it, the Bible gives a detailed list of who had whom, and who slept with whom, but we noticed a small trend that became very, very important to us.

We observed that every once in a while, they would list somebody's name, the name of their child, and then they would say something, even ever so slight, about the person. At first we thought it curious because it didn't seem to happen often, but when it did, it appeared to be important. So we concluded the logical process of the study was going to lead us to remove all of the adult's names, all of the begottens, all of the children's names, so that we could read what they were saying about these people, and what made them special.

That's when the story revealed a fascinating journey through time. What we came to realize was the Bible gives us an exact chronological storyline of humanity, the history of us as a people, and how we went from being restless wanderers to actually controlling ourselves in a social environment. In other words, the Bible's story line actually proves a human social evolution. Then, it puts a spin on it that's even more fascinating.

Well, you just have to read it yourself, but it goes through several generations.

"Lamech married two women. Their names were Adah and Zillah. Adah gave birth to Jabal *who was the father of those who lived in tents and raised livestock*. His brother's name was Jubal who was the father of all who play stringed instruments.

Then, Zillah had a son named Tubal-Cain, *who forged all kinds of tools out of bronze and iron*. Tubal-Cain's sister was Naamah."

So, think about what just happened here. It's fascinating. Take out all the names and have a look at the sub story that is developing within the family tree.

We have a restless wanderer named Cain, who's traveling about the Earth, and his profession was raising livestock. He is also familiar with farming via his late brother, Abel.

Cain understands how that system works, but now, he's out there on his own. His descendants will have to start the process all over again.

As his family begins to grow through the generations, they're wandering everywhere.

As history would have it, though we don't know how long it took, they eventually get around to mentioning someone special who is obviously important. The first person they cite was a man named Jabal, *who is the father of those who live in tents and raise livestock*.

Now why, from an economics point-of-view is this important?

It was his ingenuity that changed the world forever.

Tents are a game-changer in social evolution. Tents allow us to move. They allow us to pick up our lives and move to another place. If you have livestock, or if you've ever been around livestock, you know they do one thing very well, and that's eat. When you deplete your herds' food supply, and you're stuck without the ability to seek new resources for food, you're in trouble.

On the other hand, if you can pack up camp and move safely, then the game changes for the better. The Bible goes out of its way to introduce the gentleman named Jabal who invented tents, which allowed them to move. It also planted the seeds to create communities and live in relative safety around other humans. This meant they could constantly seek new food sources, and they could populate more rapidly. From there, social order and logistics become necessary if you are to create any type of organizational structure. That is when things start to happen for humanity, and we began to evolve as a society.

The next person the Bible found worthy to mention along with their unique contribution was a man named Jubal, created the stringed instrument.

In other words, he invented music.
What is so incredibly interesting about this is early man did not have a lot of time back then to do anything creative, especially if you are constantly on the lookout for predators and saber tooth tigers.

Think about this from their perspective, if you're wandering around, if you're a hunter-gatherer, if you're going out every day to find food and bring it back; if you're having to manage livestock, and you pick up and move on a regular basis, you essentially work from sun up to sun down. Somebody must take watch at night. You're passed out with exhaustion. You can't do anything fun or creative. You don't know how.

Yet, as a community starts to form and social evolution occurs, you begin to find free time, because within the organization, accountability and responsibility emerges. You might be in charge of the tents. Another is responsible for recon and finding areas the camp can move their livestock.

"You, you're in charge of the livestock.
You, you're in charge of berries.
You, you're in charge of fresh water."

Once all duties are organized, and everybody's not living and fending for themselves, you've got something special, and that's called free time.

Within that free time (I can imagine this being at night or around the campfire, whatever they're doing), one guy sat around and might have said, "I've got a great idea. I have been playing around with this stick, drilling holes in it and blowing air though the end. It makes a cool sound and I can play a catchy tune. I think I will play you a song."

Jubal was his name and he invented music.

(Side note: His name, Jubal, is the root word of the modern term "jubilee" which means festivities or joyous celebration.)

For the history of man and our social evolution, we went from being restless wanderers to someone getting smart and inventing the tent. This allowed us to pick up and move our livestock to the most fertile resources for food, which allowed us to construct organizational structure which gave us freedom.

Within our new found freedom, creativity emerged, and with that single spark, music was born. We can now entertain ourselves, as we create more social connections. Then, wonderful things started to happen.

As the story goes farther down the line, Zillah had a son named Tubal-Cain. Tubal-Cain was the person *who created tools out of bronze and iron*.

Within this creative period, we once again have the opportunity to do something incredible.

Tubal-Cain was able to pursue a unique path and became a metalsmith who actually created tools, using iron and bronze.

Tubal-Cain changed the world. His work began what we recognize as the emergence of the Bronze Age and the Iron Age. With tools, our ability\ty to scale, grow and mass produce became endless. It all came to be because we had social organization which freed us to become creators. Best of all, it is right there, lined out in the Old Testament, and in social and economic order.

It was perfect.

Then, as the story progresses, something cool happens once again.

For the first time in this chorological collection, they mention a woman for a reason other than bearing children. She is Tubal-Cain's sister, and her name was Naamah. What happened next, blew our minds.

 When we stepped back and realized what we were seeing in this ancient text, it took our breath away.

Naamah was special and she did something interesting, at least historically within the Christian church's folklore.

She married a man, the man's name was Noah.

This is what is so remarkable, have you ever thought to yourself, "How did Noah cut down all the trees necessary to build this ark?"

Neither did we.

We don't think normally think about the "how" as part of Noah's story, do we?

When we realized what was before us, someone had asked the question.

Where did Noah get the tools he needed to embark on such a monumental project as building a ship large enough to save the known world by hand?

It's easy if you are Noah and your wife's brother, Tubal-Cain, invented the ax, and all the tools that were necessary.
The Bible, in its beginning, tells us of a fascinating story. One of how we as humans got rejected and thrown out of our safe environment and how resilient we a species we grew to be.

In our evolution, we were able to solve certain problems. We've learned to raise livestock, but to raise livestock properly, we have to be able to move around the field and valleys. So we invented tents which soon led to social order and structure. With the community, we finally found freedom.

Freedom allows creativity to come back out into our lives after being lost leaving our safe environment (Eden). The rebirth of creativity allowed music to come into our lives. With music, you have social bonding, and the opportunity for more creative people to step in and begin what we know as the Bronze and the Iron Age. We began to make tools, which conveniently opened the door for Naamah to marry a man named Noah, who would need those tools to save the human race. At least that's how the story goes.

The Bible teaches us about social evolution but unfortunately, it's in a long and boring part of the book which seems to drag on forever. It is easy to understand why most people never get through it. For those who do drudge through the begottens and seek answers by asking "why", all the other stories will start to make sense.

 The Bible is the history of man, and it has a beginning, middle and an end. If you start in the beginning, you see where we're going. Best of all, you see what the Apostles saw coming.

That, to me, is probably the most fascinating story of all time.

Thinking Differently

Our goal at The Perfect Plan is for you to be intrigued enough by Marketing33AD to go back and relook at some of these famous stories and realize, "there really is more to it". We hope you begin to question traditional thought by asking "Is there something else that's out there?" and find a new fascination as an adult reading the greatest story ever told.

What I'm going to introduce to you is a lot of fun if you are willing to think differently. It's a story that most people know, or at least you've seen in a movie here or there.

The next story we will focus on in Marketing33AD is about the temptation of Christ. Before we begin, let's look at this man named Jesus. He is the one with a smile on his face.

Most people are familiar with the story of his birthday. He's born with a great deal of fanfare, a super nova star in heaven, three wise men and a few angles in the fields providing news to the shepherds, but that's just the beginning. There's a backstory based on how and why he decided to show up in our timeline of history.

Church tradition has it set up that God was running heaven pretty well back in the day, and he had a solid group of people around him. There was an organizational structure which included leadership with a hierarchy and purpose.

A legend has it, one of God's top commanders, a "senior executive" comes up to him and expresses his desire for "a bigger piece of the pie".

"I have worked hard" he says, "and I feel it is time for you to reward me with meaningful equity in this deal." In other words, I want to be on the same level as you, i.e. I want to rule part of the universe.

God's answer was simple, "No".

"That's not going to happen," says God. "This is a family business."

This guy, the bold one who asked for equity, has a name. His friends call him "Louie" which is short for Lucifer.

After his rejection from God, Louie decides, he doesn't like the path his career was taking and to start his own shop.

Literally, their partnership, their friendship, everything they had together, is broken up. Lucifer leaves Heaven with a bunch of other disgruntled team members who feel his vision is better than their bosses (which happens routinely in business today). So Lucifer leaves God's family business, wanting to start his own here on Earth. The only issue is Louie has an attitude problem and he's pissed.

Let us now leap forward a few billion years.

God is looking down at third planet form the sun, where Louie set up shop, and realizes they are losing a significant market share on Earth. The people, they are off track. God attempted to help in the past and event sent good leaders to right their course (which is in the Bible's book of Judges). He even sent people, whom provided a vision for their future (the prophets who were mentioned throughout the Old Testament).

The bottom line was simple, God knew it was not working, so he sent his Son down to clean it up. His son had been trained for this role and spent a few millennia tuning his skills. He was ready for the task. Let's just see what happens.
So God sends Jesus down to Earth with a new assignment: get humanity back on track and regain any market share the family business might have lost to Louie and his team.

The way the Bible tells the story, God sends Jesus down in the form of a man. His philosophy was simple: "If you're going to relate to your market, you've got to do it the way they do it and understand it. Forget however we exist in heaven today. You're going to live as one of them."

The original storytellers build a beautiful storyline. They display an enormous amount of time and effort to tell you how and where Jesus was born. We as readers, need to experience their words again, and focus both chronologically and genealogically on their meaning. It was all-important to the stories original audience to hear the narrative in the same consistent manner as they had learned the other parts of "the book". That is why we, as modern learners, need to read the Bible from the beginning. It makes more sense and purposely tells the story in a beautiful and magical way.

The Jesus story is an interesting narrative of a child, his family, and their struggles. Yet quickly and without hesitation, the story leaps to the child (Jesus) becoming an adult just before he is to take over his Father's firm.

For some reason, the Bible tells us in the book of Matthew, that Jesus volunteers to visit Louie, the devil, as we now know him prior to starting his role on Earth. If you've read or heard this story before, it's attractive and interesting, but at Marketing33AD, we want to challenge you to rethink what you know about it.

The Sunday school version that most people grow up learning tells us that Jesus wanders into the wilderness, or the desert, for forty days and for forty nights. He fasts, which means he chooses not to eat. Then, in the height of his weakness and hunger, he finds himself toe-to-toe with the story's classical villain, the ultimate bad guy himself: Lucifer.

Then, the devil, Lucifer, begins to speak with Jesus offering items specifically designed to tempt him.

This is where we started reminiscing about over the classical "Sunday School" version before we said to ourselves, "Let's read this story again, and think about it a different way."

The Temptation of Christ

Matthew Chapter 4 (Translation from the New International Version, the numbers represent the verse within the chapter for reference)

1.Then Jesus was led by the Spirit into the wilderness to be tempted by the devil. 2 After fasting forty days and forty nights, he was hungry. 3 The tempter came to him and said, "If you are the Son of God, tell these stones to become bread."

4 Jesus answered, "It is written: 'Man shall not live on bread alone, but on every word that comes from the mouth of God.'"

5 Then the devil took him to the holy city and had him stand on the highest point of the temple· 6 "If you are the Son of God", he said, "throw yourself down. For it is written:

"'He will command his angels concerning you, and they will lift you up in their hands, so that you will not strike your foot against a stone.'"

7 Jesus answered him, "It is also written: 'Do not put the Lord your God to the test.'"

8 Again, the devil took him to a very high mountain and showed him all the kingdoms of the world and their splendor. 9 "All this I will give you," he said, "if you will bow down and worship me."

10 Jesus said to him, "Away from me, Satan! For it is written: 'Worship the Lord your God, and serve him only.'"

11 Then the devil left him, and angels came and attended him.

Now, that is the classical text from which the Sunday school version is taught, but it fails to go deep and explain the "human" side of the story.

Traditionally, we get this vision of Jesus crawling through the desert, almost like the guy in the old movies stuck in a desert sandstorm, before he finally pulls himself up to see the devil standing there before him. There's a hint of a hallucination going on in Jesus head, and if you're watching those old movies, the devil says, "If you're so hungry, why don't turn these stones to bread." Jesus said, "That's not how you do it."

Then the devil says, "Look at me and I'll show you all my kingdoms." Jesus once again says, "No".

The devil then says, "Just come over here. You can be on the team. It's written here, your dad's not going to let anything happen to you." Again, Jesus said, "No." Then, Jesus starts his ministry.
Pretty simple story to the common reader, or is it?

At Marketing33AD, we had a simple question that seemed obvious, yet we had not heard it asked before.

Why did Jesus do it?

Why in the world would someone who's supposed to be the most enlightened man on the planet, who was sent down from God himself, willingly do what he did?

Why would he walk around for forty days in the desert, just to prove something?

Why would he weaken himself and then go toe-to-toe with the devil?

It just didn't make sense.

As we started digging through the story, we realized that there was more to it than we were taught in Sunday School. Originally we were just receiving the story as children, which is how we were programmed to absorb the message. Now, it is time to read it as adults.

When we began our review we wanted to know why Jesus was tempted, and what was the purpose. That is when we realized that we might be programed to think a certain way based on the stories description. Even though the chapter heading was "The Temptation of Christ", we had to wonder if the title was translated correctly, or if it was ever there to begin with. That is when it hit us.

We quickly realized that the highest probability fell on other understanding that Jesus wasn't being tempted at all.

Jesus was actually the tempter.

I challenge you to go back and read the chapter again from a different perspective.

Let's discuss a few key points.

First, we don't know if forty days and forty nights is a metaphor, because it repeats itself and occurs over and over in the Bible. The number 40 appears consistently within the "literature" of the Bible's storyline so there must be a reason for its artistic interpretation. Whether it is literally forty days of sunrises or it is a metaphor meant to stress the meaning of commitment and time, we might never know for sure, but we do know, at minimum, he skipped lunch that day.

Jesus is clearly a little bit hungry, he's a bit weakened, but he has the fortitude to go face-to-face with his dad's old partner, Lucifer. This had to be a daunting task in itself. Lucifer, the guy who left Jesus' father's firm to start his own, is the very guy from whom God himself sent Jesus down to try and win back

Earths market share. That very person was standing before Jesus and in all likelihood is still a bit pissy about how everything went down all those years ago.

As we relook at the narrative, Jesus is sitting with Lucifer, and they are having a conversation. This is where we realize our preset perception was wrong.

This wasn't a temptation.

This was a job interview.

Connect the dots: why would Jesus, the day before he was supposed to start his career and fulfil his life's mission, go to meet with his dad's old partner, who is now head of the competing firm?

That makes no sense unless Jesus had a well-orchestrated plan.

Lucifer, obviously, accepts him into his "office" and immediately says to Jesus, "Hey look, kid, here's the deal. I've seen you. I have watched you grow up and I know the work you are capable of achieving. You are without a doubt your "father's son". In fact, you are so good, I would like for you to come on board with our firm as start today as the senior Vice President of Sales and Marketing. It is the most important department in this organization."

Then as Lucifer reaches to the ground and picks up a rock, he says to Jesus "In fact, you're so good at sales and marketing, you could convince the people of Earth that this stone is actually a loaf of bread, and they will actually buy it. That is awesome. You are so good; you will dominate the market when you are over here working for me."

Jesus looked at him and simply says, "No thanks, that's not how I was taught to do business. You don't live by bread alone, and you certainly don't sell bad products."

Upon hearing Jesus, Louie begins upping the ante.

Lucifer smiles at Jesus and he says, "Hey look, this is a simple deal and a great opportunity for you. Just come on over to our firm, and we will figure it out as we go along. In fact, I've known your dad forever. I've got this old email here, a memo that's written down and it basically says your dad will always take you back. In fact, he even says he will watch over you and won't even let you stub your toe. So come on over. Enjoy the firm. If it doesn't work out, then you can leave. We'll part as friends, and you can always go back and work for your dad. Again, it says it right here, you can always come home."

Then, Jesus looked at him and said, "You know, that paper might be correct, but I have witnessed my father change his mind a few times. What I have learned through the years I that you should never tempt him. He is the boss and I have seen him change his mind. He might throw away that old email and write a new one".

Then, Lucifer knowing he is running out of cards to play, says to Jesus, "Hey look, I totally dig it, kid. We all know you're better than sales and marketing. You're better than any middle management-type position, and you need a long term guarantee. This is a big decision for us both, so I'm going to go ahead and make you President of the company. Come here and see your new world as I see it. Let me show you something special."

Then, Lucifer takes Jesus up to the highest level, the roof of his building, the highest part of the temple, and he shows him all the kingdoms of the world which report directly to him.

Lucifer says, "Look at all of these wonderful places I control." In other words, "Look at our facilities within the Han dynasty in China. Look at what's happening in the Peruvian nations. Check out the emerging markets in what we will one day call the "Americas."

He goes on telling Jesus, "Look what's happening with the Barbarians to the Northeast of Rome. Look at all these kingdoms around the world that I just so happen to have control over and who respectfully report to me. It's all going to be yours now, kid. But here's the deal: You're the new President of my company, but I'm still the Chairman of the Board. So, all you've got to do is just make sure you pass everything by me before you make any big decisions. Don't get me wrong, you are the President, but you still work for me. We are going to run this whole thing together."

Jesus looked at him and said once again, "No. That's not what I was sent here to do."

Then, Jesus abruptly leaves Lucifer, and God sends his assistants, the angels, to care for him. The very next day, Jesus begins his work rebuilding the world and regaining their family market share.

Think about this. Why did he do it? Why did he go and spend time with Lucifer himself?

Our thoughts became clear.

What if the title was wrong or we were simply reading it incorrectly?
What if Jesus wasn't being tempted, but he himself was the tempter?

Was Jesus simply going to visit his competition and say, "Hey, what've you got? What are you up to?" We don't know for sure if Lucifer extended the invitation to meet and interview Jesus, or if Jesus did it himself. The story never tells us, nor does it tell us if Jesus was actually entertaining the idea of working for the competing firm. Better yet, (and much more probable) what if Jesus is simply on a recon mission.

What if Jesus wanted to know a little bit more about the firm he was going to be compete with.

It happens every day in business. People get job offers from the competition. They go to meet and experience the interview process. They're mostly curious in a way, because the great performers and leaders just want to know what's happening on the other side in order to combat their game plan. For the good-guy-team, this is of little risk because if they're in a good environment, the good leaders and performers always stay.

Jesus knew what his mission was, and he never doubted. Nor was he ever "tempted." He knew he was sent there by God, and by no means, had he any intent of going to work for Lucifer. Jesus was smart and he simply wanted to know what the other team's secret was that enabled them to gain such market penetration so quickly on Earth.

Think about it this way.

Here's the bad guy, Lucifer, and he's had a big run for a long time. His market share is dominant. Now, here comes his ex-partner's kid, who is truly gifted, who he knows is going to make an impact, and he is doing everything he can to get him to come work for him. Lucifer will do anything to keep him from fulfilling the mission that his Father sent him to do.

Thankfully, Jesus was smart enough to say, "No thanks. That's not why I'm here."

When studying the temptation of Christ, we have to ask, "Who is really the tempter in the story?"

I think it might have been Jesus himself, not the other way around. At a bare minimum, it was, as we originally thought, a job interview.

Ponder this thought when you read the Bible as an adult. When you ask why, you might find these characters are no different from you and it is more "real" than you thought.

So what can we learn from this story?

Temptation can go both ways and it is not always a bad thing, especially when you have a plan.

Jesus Wept

As we explored the proof of social evolution in the book of Genesis, we realized how important it is to see mankind grow, learn, and become creative. The Bible clearly tells us that we are made in the image (better word for translation is "reflection") of God, and if we believe God is the great creator, then we must accept that we are built to be creators ourselves. S we read through this great book, the history of man is revealed before your eyes. While it might seem boring at first, if you hang in there and boldly question the 'why' of the story, then you'll find it is really interesting.

The Bible tells the story of us, and proves our own mindset has been evolving from the beginning.

What's really cool about the book of Genesis and our exponential growth in social evolution is that you cannot go back and mix up the order in which it was written in hopes of making it work any better. In fact, just the opposite is true. The story line as it is presented had to be in the exact chronological sequence of events in which it was told or the story will fall apart for future, more educated civilizations (that's you and me, by the way). The beauty is in its order.

A perfect order.

For thousands, or tens of thousands, or millions of years, we have shared these stories verbally at night and over campfires by our tents to each other. It is nothing short of a miracle, it all stayed together.

Someone must have a master plan in mind in order to make it work. We can see this as the novel moves through time and into the modern age. There before our eye, just in time, as the novel finally begins to unfold, our hero arrives.

Foretold throughout the Bible but seemingly random and innocent as though out of nowhere, the emergence of an unlikely character named Jesus defines the story.

We follow him from birth to adolescence before we suddenly discover him wandering in the desert as an adult heading toward a job interview.

Our hope in writing this book is that you, as an adult, can now look at that storyline a little bit differently and say, "You know what, the most enlightened man on the planet would not have done it the way we are taught he did it. He never needed to be tempted in order to find enlightenment. He was already there. So it is up to us as adults to change the way we view the narrative and ask, what if he, Jesus, was actually the tempter and did things on his terms? What if he, in his attempt to learn the truth about the other side, actually began the process necessary to save the world?

We will never know unless we start to ask "why?"

As the temptation story concludes, Jesus begins his mission, and several more beautiful stories begin to unfold. In future editions of this book, you'll be able to learn more, but in order for you to continue toward your own Perfect Plan, I want to share with you one of my favorite of the "Jesus" stories, referred to as "Jesus Wept."

Now, every kid who grew up in a Christian or parochial school knows by memory this one special verse from the Bible's Book of John. At school, when you're told to go home and memorize a verse from the Bible, every kid knows where to search because it's the shortest verse in the entire book. It's just two simple words. It literally says:

"Jesus wept."

It's a fantastic story about Jesus' friend, (or maybe his cousin according to some genealogy scholars), whose name was Lazarus.

Lazarus was a person who had recently passed away, for reasons unknown to the reader. As the story unfolds, Jesus is summoned to his grave, where he went, met the family, and he cried. Hence the verse "Jesus wept".

In the Sunday school version, you've got Jesus arriving to the funeral a few days after the death of Lazarus, where he is confronted by a group of mourners near the grave, most of whom are women. Because he missed the formal funeral itself, the women are all heartbroken, so Jesus begins to cry.

Jesus then does the most amazing thing, and in pure compassion, commands Lazarus to wake and come out of the tomb, thus he raises Lazarus from the dead. He says, "Lazarus come out," and he "heals" him. It's all a great thing, but Jesus is saddened and he's crying, or so the story goes.

As you might imagine by now, when we read through the story depicted in the Bible's Book of John, we had a very different perspective.

Our question was simple.

Why would Jesus cry?

It was not simply "why _did_ Jesus cry?" but "why _would_ he cry?"

Please read the excerpt below from John's complete book that focuses on the story of Jesus and Lazarus. Please read it twice, once as you have read it before, and again with an open mind.

John Chapter 11

The Death of Lazarus

1. Now a man named Lazarus was sick. He was from Bethany, the village of Mary and her sister Martha. ² (This Mary, whose brother Lazarus now lay sick, was the same one who poured perfume on the Lord and wiped his feet with her hair.)³ So the sisters sent word to Jesus, "Lord, the one you love is sick."

⁴ When he heard this, Jesus said, "This sickness will not end in death. No, it is for God's glory so that God's Son may be glorified through it." *⁵ Now Jesus loved Martha and her sister and Lazarus. ⁶ So when he heard that Lazarus was sick, he stayed where he was two more days,* ⁷ and then he said to his disciples, "Let us go back to Judea."

⁸ "But Rabbi," they said, "a short while ago the Jews there tried to stone you, and yet you are going back?"

⁹ Jesus answered, "Are there not twelve hours of daylight? Anyone who walks in the daytime will not stumble, for they see by this world's light. ¹⁰ It is when a person walks at night that they stumble, for they have no light."

¹¹ After he had said this, he went on to tell them, "Our friend Lazarus has fallen asleep; but I am going there to wake him up."
¹² His disciples replied, "Lord, if he sleeps, he will get better." ¹³ Jesus had been speaking of his death, but his disciples thought he meant natural sleep.

¹⁴ So then he told them plainly, "Lazarus is dead, ¹⁵ and for your sake I am glad I was not there, so that you may believe. But let us go to him."

¹⁶ Then Thomas (also known as Didymus) said to the rest of the disciples, "Let us also go, that we may die with him."

Jesus Comforts the Sisters of Lazarus

17 On his arrival, Jesus found that Lazarus had already been in the tomb for four days. **18** Now Bethany was less than two miles from Jerusalem, **19** and many Jews had come to Martha and Mary to comfort them in the loss of their brother. **20** When Martha heard that Jesus was coming, she went out to meet him, but Mary stayed at home.

21 "Lord," Martha said to Jesus, "if you had been here, my brother would not have died. **22** But I know that even now God will give you whatever you ask."

23 Jesus said to her, "Your brother will rise again."

24 Martha answered, "I know he will rise again in the resurrection at the last day."

25 Jesus said to her, "I am the resurrection and the life. The one who believes in me will live, even though they die; **26** and whoever lives by believing in me will never die. Do you believe this?"

27 "Yes, Lord," she replied, "I believe that you are the Messiah, the Son of God, who is to come into the world."

28 After she had said this, she went back and called her sister Mary aside. "The Teacher is here," she said, "and is asking for you." **29** When Mary heard this, she got up quickly and went to him. **30** Now Jesus had not yet entered the village, but was still at the place where Martha had met him. **31** When the Jews who had been with Mary in the house, comforting her, noticed how quickly she got up and went out, they followed her, supposing she was going to the tomb to mourn there.

32 When Mary reached the place where Jesus was and saw him, she fell at his feet and said, "Lord, if you had been here, my brother would not have died."

33 When Jesus saw her weeping, and the Jews who had come along with her also weeping, he was deeply moved in spirit and troubled. **34** "Where have you laid him?" he asked. "Come and see, Lord," they replied.

35 Jesus wept.

36 Then the Jews said, "See how he loved him!"
37 But some of them said, "Could not he who opened the eyes of the blind man have kept this man from dying?"

38 Jesus, once more deeply moved, came to the tomb. It was a cave with a stone laid across the entrance. **39** "Take away the stone," he said. "But, Lord," said Martha, the sister of the dead man, "by this time there is a bad odor, for he has been there four days."

40 Then Jesus said, "Did I not tell you that if you believe, you will see the glory of God?"

41 So they took away the stone. Then Jesus looked up and said, "Father, I thank you that you have heard me. **42** I knew that you always hear me, but I said this for the benefit of the people standing here, that they may believe that you sent me."

43 When he had said this, Jesus called in a loud voice, "Lazarus, come out!"

44 The dead man came out, his hands and feet wrapped with strips of linen, and a cloth around his face.

Jesus said to them, "Take off the grave clothes and let him go."

As you consider the story, I encourage you to read it again. On the second pass, you should focus on the fact that Jesus created the situation that made that scenario happen. In other words, Jesus was in total control of how this story would unfold.

He knew what was going to happen and the timing it would take to maximize the impact of what he needed to do.

Ironically, as sad as the story might be, there's even a little bit of comedy in it. There's somewhat of a 'Jerry Seinfeld' comedic moment between the women and Jesus., There is a "ribbing" that occurs by the women implying "if you could heal the blind man then certainly you could have done this". I can just see them on the streets of New York, in a Seinfeld episode with Jerry, Kramer and Elaine as they pick on George for not being where he should have been and being late.
Let's go back and look at this story again:

To put the story in perspective, Jesus was on the other side of town, fewer than two miles away when he had been told several times that his friend/cousin, Lazarus, was dying. He was needed to come help them and to heal Lazarus.

Jesus literally takes his time getting there. He does not rush to help Lazarus out. He basically sits around, and when he does show up, it is long after Lazarus had died (four days later, to be exact).

When he walks up to the crowd, the first person who comes out to meet him was Mary, the sister of Lazarus, and she is crying. This is where the story truly begins.

Again, keep this in perspective. Jesus had been told Lazarus was dying. He had been asked to come help, but he purposefully did not. Jesus took his time, Lazarus dies, but then, after a few days, he goes to the town and the first people that come running up to him are the family.

"When Mary reached the place where Jesus was and saw Him, she fell at his feet and said, 'Lord,'" (which is a title of respect.) "'If you'd been here, my brother would not have died.' But then Jesus saw her weeping, and the Jews who had come along were also weeping.

He was deeply moved in spirit and troubled. 'Where have you laid him?' he said. 'Come and see,' she replied."

Then, Jesus wept.

Upon seeing Jesus begin to cry, the women in the crowd said to each other, "See how He loved him." But some of them said, "Could you not have been here when he died? You could've been here. You could open the eyes of the blind man, but you couldn't keep Lazarus from dying."

"Jesus was once more deeply moved, and He came to the tomb, a cave with a stone laid across the entrance. He said, 'Take away the stone.' 'But Lord,' said Martha, the sister of the dead man. 'By this time, there's a bad odor, and he's been there for three days.'

Jesus said, '*Did I tell you that if you believe, you'll see the glory of God?*'

So she took away the stone, and Jesus looked up and said, 'Father,' (in other words, he prays)

"'Thank you that you've heard me. I know that You always hear me. *I say this for the benefit of the people standing here, that they might believe that You sent me.*'

Then, Jesus called out *in a loud voice*, 'Lazarus, come out.' Lazarus comes out. His hands, his feet, and his face were still wrapped in the linen burial cloth.

Jesus said (with emphasis), '*Take the grave clothes off of him and let him go.*'"

Now again, reading as a Sunday School story, we look back on it, and we say to ourselves, in Sunday School order:

- He got there.
- He missed Lazarus' death.
- All of the people were mourning.
- Jesus is sad so he starts crying.
- Jesus is really mourning Lazarus.
- Jesus says, "Okay, okay. I'm sorry I missed it, but I'll heal him now".
- He tells them to "Move the stone."
- Ironically, the crowd starts to have second thoughts. They're saying, "Whoa. Wait a minute. It's going to smell pretty bad here if we open this thing. He's been dead for a few days."
- Then, Jesus says a prayer.
- He says to move the stone again.
- They move it.
- Lazarus comes out.
- Jesus says, "Take the clothes off of him."
- Everyone is happy, Lazarus is alive once again and healed.

Now, as an adult, think about it again and ask yourself "Why?"

Why would Jesus have taken his time?

Even better yet, if he knew all of this, why would he have cried?

Why did he not mention healing Lazarus in his prayer to God?

Why did he not run up to Lazarus when he came out of the grave?

Why was Jesus not over joyed to see Lazarus?

Go back with these questions in mind, and read the story from a different point of view.

In the beginning, Mary comes up to him and says, "Lord, if you'd been here, my brother would not have died." When Jesus saw her weeping, the storyteller clearly tells the reader that Jesus was *"deeply moved in spirit and troubled."*
"Where have you laid him?" Jesus asked, and then she said, "Come and see."

Think about it this way. Jesus was deeply moved in spirit, and he is troubled. Deep in his core, there is something wrong. Something is bothering him. The storyteller, John, emphasizes Jesus is "troubled", yet he never says he is "sad."
Then, while he is deeply troubled, Jesus began to cry.

Jesus wept.

From a storyline frame of reference, that is an odd place for that to happen. Normally it would have occurred upon the news of his death, or when he reached Mary as a comforter and cried with her, but he didn't.

He simply wept when he became troubled.

What's interesting within this entire dialogue is the Bible doesn't say that he was ever crying for Lazarus. The women in the crowd looked at him and said, "Oh, see how He loved him?"

All the people that are around are just assuming that Jesus cried because he's mourning for Lazarus, but again, the Bible doesn't say that. It says he's troubled. So what does that mean?

Then, "He could open the eyes of a blind man, but he couldn't keep save Lazarus from dying?"

Now, they're saying, "Oh, you can do the 'heal the blind man magic trick', but you can't do this." They're really kind of beating him up a little and taking it out on him. Then the story reiterates that Jesus, once more, was deeply moved and he walked to the tomb.

Then, without any prompting, Jesus prayed. I want you to really look very closely at what he said in his prayer and focus on the purpose of the communication to God.

First of all, he says to the crowd, "Did I tell you that if you believe, you'll see the glory of God?" He's talking to the crowd. If *you* believe, *you* will see the glory of God, but he's still sad and troubled.

He then looked up and said his prayer, addressing God as "Father," reminding us of their relationship.

He begins his prayer with an attitude of gratitude; "I thank you that you've heard me.
Thank you that you're listening to me. Thank you that you took my call." He says, "I know that you always hear me, but *I've said this for the benefit of the people standing here*, that they may believe that You sent me."

Look at what he's saying. "I say this for the benefit of those around me, that they may believe that You sent me."

He does not pray for Lazarus.

He doesn't pray at all for Lazarus.

He's praying and saying, "Thank you, God, for taking my call. Thank you for having a moment to speak to me. I'm asking you do this for these other people."

He never, ever mentions Lazarus.

Then, the writer tell us this:

"Jesus called out with a loud voice", not just a soft voice, a loud voice, a commanding voice, "Lazarus, come out."

Then, the dead man came out with his head and his feet wrapped in cloth, and Jesus said, "Take off the grave clothes and let him go."

What's interesting in that is he could've easily just said something nice. He could've smiled. He could've done the things that we've grown to love this guy for, but he was still deeply troubled.

He prayed to God, yet he did not pray for Lazarus.

He prayed for the other people to believe, and while being troubled and intently focused, he screamed, "Lazarus, come out."

Here lies the key to the entire story.

He was actually upset that he had to ask Lazarus to come out of the grave.

Jesus was rattled with discuss at this point.

Then, he looks at the crowd, and he says, "Take off the grave clothes and let him go."

When you go back and read this story again, think to yourself, "Wait a minute. You mean Jesus never prayed for Lazarus? Jesus never talked about Lazarus? The same Jesus that was troubled in his spirit, prayed for the other people and not for Lazarus.

What do you think that was really about?

This is where it finally hit us. It was about something more beautiful than what this story could've ever been taught in Sunday school.

You see, Jesus wasn't crying because he was mourning. Jesus knew Lazarus was going to die. Jesus had known he died whenever it had happened.

Jesus certainly wasn't crying because the people around him were crying, they were actually poking and insulting him in a back-handed manner.

Yet, Jesus was troubled.
He was not mourning. He was troubled.

He was troubled for one thing, and one thing only.

Jesus wept because of what he had to ask Lazarus to do.

Jesus did the unthinkable and asked Lazarus to leave heaven and return to earth, just so others might believe.

You see, to help those other people, Jesus, as a leader, had to do the unimaginable. He had to put Lazarus in harm's way by asking Lazarus to leave heaven and to come back to Earth.

In other words, Lazarus was dead and whatever faith you are, if you believe that there is a heaven, then Lazarus was there.

Lazarus was dead yet living again in heaven amongst the coolest and the greatest glory of God, but Jesus had to say, "Oh, wait a minute. My bad. We're just kidding. You've got to leave this paradise. You have to leave this eternal bliss and this wonderful place, this purest endowment of joy, and you've got to come back here to Earth, just to prove to those other people the point of my mission."

That's why Jesus was crying.
That should make anyone cry.

Jesus was not crying because he was mourning. Jesus was crying because of what he had to ask Lazarus to do; to leave heaven and come back to Earth just to prove a point to somebody who just couldn't believe.

Jesus as the ultimate leader, even when experiencing an immense and troubled spirit, was able to do what was necessary.

As a leader, sometimes you have to put people in harm's way. You have to ask them to do something for a greater good, even if they don't want to do it. Jesus taught us that a leader can be very moved and troubled, but they will do what they have to do.

Jesus wasn't mourning. Jesus was broken and troubled that he had to ask Lazarus to do something unimaginable in order to serve others, so that the movement would continue on.

That is a fascinating story.

That is something Sunday School might have missed.

The Path to Your Perfect Plan...

Our mission and desire at the Perfect Plan is for you to pick up and read the Bible as an adult.

But guess what? It's a hard read sometimes, so I suggest you get the Bible in a language you understand. We recommend you try an edition called NIV, or New International Version. That's my favorite. It is written in modern English, but there are multiple translations available to suit your reading style. Get what's best for you, and start reading it.

As you begin, you must get through what might appear at first to be the more difficult and boring sections. I know there's a lot of 'begottens' going on, but that's ok, they're just having sex and populating the planet. So, look at the cool things they mention about certain people and ask yourself:

- What did they do?
- Did they invent music?
- Did they invent tents?
- Did they invent iron?
- Who are they related to?
- Does their name appear later in the timeline as well?

Just the idea that guy sister was married to Noah's, and he could not have built the Ark without him, is incredible. It is also the beginning of the Iron Age and would change the world forever.

There are fascinating, things that are in there if you look for it and you are not afraid to ask why.

As you start to read through the Bible's main story line, you see this beautiful, epic story begin to emerge. You think Harry Potter and Star Wars is good? Wait until you read this book!

It's a story of an agape love that God has for the people. It is a love story between a father and his son, between a creator and his people. As the story moves ahead you're exposed to the richest stories in the history of humanity. As the story unfolds, a clash begins to brew between good and evil as everything is pushed to the brink, but that's when the hero arrives.

God sent his Son down to say, "Hey look, we need to clean things up a bit and get some of our market share back. Let me see what's going on, and let me know how I can help. All you have to do is ask."

If you read it as an adult, and take the Sunday School images out of your head, there's a lot you can learn from it, and there's a lot you will see differently. Whether it was a job interview, or a leader asking somebody to do something for somebody else, it was always the right thing to do.

There are more leadership stories in the Bible than anywhere else in history.

There are more marketing and sales stories and all the business books combined.

There are history stories, love stories, villains, heroes and even a few mystical beasts than any fantasy novel could imagine.

It is, without question, the greatest story ever told.

Here's a little secret.

It is better as an adult.

In time, you might ask yourself, how can I help carry the movement forward?

Well, it is easier than you might imagine, and this is only the beginning of your special journey, your Perfect Plan.

If we can ever help you, please let us know.

Reach out. If you just want to have a few minutes of a conversation to say, "Hey, I'm struggling with this. I just need someone to talk with and help me understand it better," we're happy to speak with you.

If you want to explore opportunities for additional lessons, either by video or in person, just let us know. We can come onsite to your small group, your church, or your business, and can go deeper in these fascinating stories. We can help you learn how they apply to your unique path.

We are honored to serve you and to help you.

If you want to seek advanced knowledge, and get into the Perfect Plan, we are here for you.

The Perfect Plan is a 15-course study on what the most impactful people do differently. It is their formula for success. Conveniently, it's exactly the same formula as what's written in the Bible, whether they knew it or not.

The Perfect Plan is about mindset, teamwork and action. It is about how you can become a better leader and get your mind and heart in the right place as a servant. We discuss modern impact performers as well as Biblical principles and truths. We learn in a way the Bible was meant to be studied, as an adult.

Best of all, as you go through the course, it is important for you that we prove it scientifically, and we show you how to apply it. As you go forward you will be equipped to say, "Now, I get it. My heart and my mind are in the right place. How do I go out there and cultivate people so that they can go out and spread servant leadership faster than I could have by myself?"

That is the amazing part of the process. It's interactive, and not only teaches you how to lead, but how to cultivate people as well.

Finally, in the last five sessions, we go beyond the Perfect Plan, beyond the Cultivation Rule to explore the truth of why we are here and what we are meant to do. We discover your purpose.

You will find an inspired change in the future of your organization, of you as a person, of your family, and of your community, just by serving others. The interaction is amazing, and the growth you will experience, personally and professionally, is at times, divine.

Thank you. I hope you enjoyed this, and if there's anything we can do for you, please let us know.

Don

Here's The Path to Your Perfect Plan...

You already know the stories from your childhood. They may have seemed simple then, but looking back it is easy to realize something is missing. That's why we decided to look back as adults and ask "what really happened?"

This book is dedicated to curious people.

As you read and discover how these priceless stories you might have learned as a child apply to your life today. You will begin your quest for life's Perfect Plan.

Here are three ways we can help you right now...

Option 1: Commit to reading a modern English edition of the Bible as if it is a novel, beginning to end. If that feels intimidating, give us a call at **770-225-4909**. We will do everything we can to help you out and make it an inspiring process.

Option 2: Ask us about joining us for a small workshop where we help you make the connection between the stories in the Bible and how it applies to your life today.

Option 3: Purchase our online video series and small group study materials. You can find out more information at **www.Marketing33ADtoday.com**.

Most people live their life with childhood stories, wondering why nothing ever came of it.

Now, with our help, you can look back at those precious stories as an adult, apply them to your life as it is today, and go change the world.

Visit **www.Marketing33ADtoday.com** to get started.

"For I know the plans I have for you," declares the Lord, "plans to prosper you and not to harm you, plans to give you hope and a future."
– Jeremiah 29:11

www.ingramcontent.com/pod-product-compliance
Lightning Source LLC
LaVergne TN
LVHW010016070426
835511LV00001B/4